I0158342

OCEANS

the depths of being

Jasmine Johnston

copyright 2022 © JASMINE JOHNSTON

All rights reserved.

OCEANS

ISBN 978-0-6456950-1-4 (Paperback)

to anyone who's ever felt their feelings, and felt like they were diving into the ocean. this is for you

authors note

i wrote oceans over 2-years. she's my first book baby to hit the universe, which i never expected. oceans covers all the feelings, feeling the feelings, and discovering the deep places of ourselves can be safe and good. the feelings, the romance, the fear, the anger, the frustration, the rebellion, the wanting, the pleasure, the discovery. all of it is neutral ground — no feeling good or bad. i've had to learn to embrace them all, and you'll find all of them scattered throughout this collection. oceans follows as i deep dive into discovering my sexuality, breaking up with toxic people and places, being betrayed, feeling all the feels, seeing inequality, and falling in love. i hope the words remind you of the depths of our being — the grey, the deep, the blue, and the raging. i hope the words let you find yourself a little, too.

all my love,
jasmine.

the grey

falling

sometimes i am falling
and the only thing to catch me
is another arm on mine
the steady look in her eyes

i spend days dreaming
about what it would be like
to hold your face

of course,
i wake up.

i spend nights laying awake
the city sounds and this god damn ceiling fan
my only company

of course,
sleep evades me.

your grey eyes lit my sky brighter than the sunrise

molten gold
flowing like honey
through my core
from my chest
liquid *lust*
she pours into me

am i truly seeking you
or do i desire the muse?

am i truly seeking your eyes
or am i avoiding mine?

your eyes are the colour
of all the poems
i never wrote
and never read
your eyes are full of
all the words
magic
left unsaid
they glitter with sharp edges and
soft pillows and
they glow with all the hope
i wish i could muster

baby your eyes are oceans

do you wait for me
like i wait for you?
does seeing my name
make your fingers move?
curving around words
like they wish they were curving around you
i'll never say a single one
my fingers are phantoms without any touch
but i hope
and isn't that what keeps us going?
the hope
we feel
every time i wish i could feel
your face
but instead i see
your name.

how am i supposed to
just breathe
when you —
you knock the air right out of me

eyes meet
like a childhood romance
across the room
your gaze
both
devoured me
and
gave me back to myself
all at once

i wish i could say
it happened
because of anything else
but if i'm honest
it happened
because it's you
and i have always fallen apart
a stitch at a time
come completely undone
because of you.

you promised me you wouldn't fall in love and i breathed a sigh
of pain-filled relief when you didn't ask me to do the same.

there are wild waves that crash upon soft shores
may we learn to weather
all kinds of weather

together.

my mind wanders, straying like a cool spring breeze. my
thoughts catch on the wind and the wind, i know she carries
them to you. tell me, when i think of you, do you think of me
too? do you feel a phantom hand caress your face? did you feel
the way my heart catches on your name? when i think of you,
do you think of me too?

haunted.

i am afraid of the places
the oceans, the waves, take me
out to sea
on currents unchartered
we tumble in their flow

feelings.

i see the softness in you
your sharp eyes hide it well
but i see it and that softness is a whole fucking safety net i am
ready to dive into
like being coiled up in thick blankets
surrounded by mosquito nets and
the spring air
and flowers on the breeze
your arms around me
you awakened a hunger
a sweet like honey and
burning like flames wanting
darling darling
if i had the chance
i'd devour you entirely

grey eyes hold me
glued in place
as i fumble for the door
with hands that no longer work
they crack and crumble as
your eyes hold me
glued in place
as i fumble for my self
my god
where is the reflection
that stared back at me?

i can't see her anymore.

me in the dark
you in the quiet

you're in your head
and i can't get you out of mine

manipulation

winter surrounds us
and the cold is blistering
it chills us to the bone
are you even listening?

still,
these winds are kinder
than what you left me

nothing but tyre marks
on a cold road
from a broken heart
a missing car and a
gas tank on empty.

ice forms on black roads that
lead us out of this small town
guess this road and the cold wind and broken bones
is all we have left now

i stand on the shore
watching as days pass by and
i stand on the shore
watching.

days pass by.

sometimes grief looks like
not knowing what grief looks like

    empty
      silent.

sometimes grief looks like,
feeling the loss that you do not understand
the loss that opens caverns within you
caves in mountainsides that have not been inhabited in an age

sometimes grief looks like
not pushing away the waves, but
letting them run their course
trusting the timing of the moon

to keep them ebbing flowing peaceful wild

these waves are crashing,
moving over the rough places
until the stones are smooth to touch
until the healing starts to come

sometimes grief feels like a river opening into an ocean
in its quiet rush in its complex path
in the way we can't stop it even if we want to

the water rushes
as she moves
surges
around me
she carries me

it is as though every tear i have ever let loose
has found its way here
home, in this river
the tears fall only to *return*
to come back full circle

they come back to hold me
they come back to carry me

when the weight is too much
for me alone
when grief is pressing my shoulders down
the water
she carries me

i want to love you forever
yet a part of me,
stretching her arms
glancing bleary eyed
at this new world she's seeing
she's waking up.
i want to love you forever
but i want to love her, too

and baby, you should never have to choose.

like the waves
crash and fall
so do we
so do we

so do i.

how do i hold
all that i am
when all that i am
is shifting sand.

feel the well
let the waves rise up and
let it be
what it is meant to be
let the well
be a well

*don't be afraid to let the well be a well. don't be afraid to feel
the feelings. don't be afraid to let it all pour out, when it needs
to.*

sometimes you look at me and
it's like I am the only one in the room
and sometimes
you look at me
and i see
you are a thousand miles away.

reflections.

everything bubbles
and ricochets
and here, still water
doesn't exist
there's only soda
and crashing waves
swirling currents
and everything bubbles
and ricochets

you are the certainty amidst the storm
you are the wonder keeping my eyes wide

i am the certainty amidst the storm
i am the wonder keeping my eyes wide

the depths

feeling

maybe everything that comes alive is always meant to die.

the silence is no longer a resounding echo
bouncing off cave walls
it is now a gentle breeze
that licks at my skin and
wraps me up to
call me home to
rest

the silence is no longer a pain, it's a gift

fingers drag down
the walls of the well
trying to stop your
fall
as you descend
into the place
you would rather avoid

but
with bleeding fingertips and a heavy heart
you fall
anyway

the question is —
the question always has been —
whether it is a slow and painful descent
or a clean fall
into these deep places

the depths of yourself

so,

let go.

i feel like i have been thrown into the ocean and i know i am
supposed to be there but i have no fucking clue what to hold on
to to stay afloat and god-knows i have no idea how to swim but
also why stay afloat at all? is that not another expectation i
didn't choose? another way for me to conform to the walls that
used to hold me? imagine — i could sink fully into this place.
yes, i sense the tides shifting. not in the water around me — in
the spaces within me. i am shifting. so i stop trying to float or
swim. i dive in.

there are oceans within us
they rage
they rise
there are oceans within us
and they are calling us
deeper.

i spoke to the seas and they heard me
they whispered back
as they kissed my feet
and they,
they told me where to go.

the deep places are listening, they are speaking, listen.

the waves fill and the shores empty
the sea is always the sea

but the coastline
experiences different depths
ebbs and flows
of full and empty

*are we not all coastlines of ourselves? feeling full, feeling
empty? trust the sea to be the sea. full and empty and full and
empty. all are good.*

on a lifeboat
clinging for dear life
as the waves swell
and the currents pull
around her
holding tightly to this buoy
that won't stay upright
it falls and swells with the sea
and God knows it's a fight to breathe
tell me why do we fight
the rhythms, the currents, of life?
why is she still holding this buoy?
a floatation device
that threatens to take her life?
we have been taught for too long
that it's wrong to let go
still
all i seek
to fall into the sea
to let the waves pull me under
to let the waves pull me home
there are deeper places still, i know
and there's always beauty, in the letting go.

i'm sitting in the gardens surrounded by the sounds of nature
rivers rushing
makes me wonder
what the point is
of the city rush?
the mess of the forest floor
reminds me that
growth comes
all the time
and the "mess"
it's all life, really.
flowers are blooming
in too many colours to count
and i can see those colours
experience their mystery
why do we try to control
nature
our nature
the world of nature
when we can contemplate it
sit in it — bask in it — see it
instead?
who taught us control
over seeing?
who taught us control
over being?

the sky is threatening rain
threatening as though that wouldn't be the best damn thing
to sit here in the rain and feel the way that
life rejuvenates under drops of water
like diving naked into the sea and
the wind pushes my hair from my face
as a lover would
in a way, i suppose
she is a lover, this wind
who has wrapped herself around me and held me
as i sit here and watch the sky threaten to cover me with her
healing waters.

such stark contrast
between sunshine and the storm

what are you choosing?

maybe this is all there is.

maybe we should live like this is all there is.

i saw my reflection in the bus as it flew passed me
and i noticed for the first time how much
we stand still
held in a moment.
i saw my face
reflected in the windows of
the bus as it flew
passed me.
i stood on the sidewalk
and i watched
and i felt myself
being watched
and i wondered how many times
i had stopped and
only
watched.
both not enough
and too many
too few times i had seen myself
too many times i had stood apart to watch
and i felt it all
i saw it all in
this moment that i
saw myself.

*the lights turned green and the bus kept moving and i guess it
was a green light for me to keep moving, too.*

a flowing river lies
deep within us
somewhere below
the well we have been taught to trust

there's more in you than the shallows, baby

dead branches are part of life
dead branches
make room for life

the dead makes way for the living
why are you holding the parts of you that died?
when you could make new rooms,
usher in new life?

sweet and safe rolled off my tongue
faster than the sweetness, the safety
could even be absorbed
before i realised,
i had never realised —
i don't want
sweet
or
safe.

don't sweep another dream
another feeling
under the rug
because it's safer
because it's easier
because it's more comfortable
because they tell you to.

take the rug
from the floor
hang it outside
give it some air
and let your floors be bare

show the world the dreams you're feeling.

there's a place by the water
where the stars dangle from the trees
little golden orbs
lighting up the night
baby you should see it
the way the stars collide with the earth
it's like they have been searching and now
they're here
and they're still searching
like they got stuck in this familiar place and are clinging to it
hoping that maybe
the unfamiliar, wonder, might find them
i watch these magic encased trees
holding the wonder of the universe
on their branches
and i wonder — are we not the same?
aren't we all like the stars on the trees?
don't we feel the pull of new
of "something" out there
and yet we stay in place
tied to little ropes of our own comfort
we light up and pray that wonder would cross our path
we sit in our four walls but we hunger for the whole fucking
sky

and my god
do we hunger for change

i dream of days
long forgotten
and wake
with their presence
lingering
on my skin

like salt after the sea

i'm here trying to describe the way the city lights bring me back to life

in the aching
in the quiet
in the void
know
hope can rise
peace will come
you are not the aching
you are not the quiet
you are not the void
you are oceans of wonder

i see the dark of night and
it reminds me
again and again and again
that even when all is dark and night surrounds us
still,
the light of the stars and the moon break through.

watch — she is rising.

are you broken?
really?
or
is everyone telling you that you are
broken,
is their ideas of what's broken,
making you think
you're broken?

how do you break the sea baby? we are all fractured and
whole.

i wrote a thousand words
and none were enough
none were enough
none were enough
until one day
all were enough.

these words are healing.

i dated a boy once,
who didn't understand poetry
as though poetry isn't an entire language
that the whole damn universe uses
as though it didn't matter
that this boy decided
the language of the universe to be
irrelevant
the universe doesn't speak to us
in words we can comprehend
instead she chooses
tantalising tastes and memories
whispers of words our bodies have forgotten
i dated a boy who didn't understand poetry
and i wonder if that's wasn't the universe
reminding me
you've gotta find the people who speak your language
you've gotta seek the people who speak my language
you've gotta remember baby
that poetry is the language of the soul
the language of the body
the language of love
and all of those places
are where you'll find me.

i find you like a river finds its course
n a t u r a l l y
water flows and
currents change and
in no two days are we the same
like stones
smoothed by years of movement
glittering in the sunlight
she shines through

and when i see her
everything
just
stops.

a glance in the river,
a nod to my reflection —
i found myself when i found you.

i am learning about myself
as though for the first time
i am peeking through
the grief, the pain
and glittering eyes
meet my reflection
am i trapped in this mirror
or am I breaking through?

i think it's time for breakthrough baby.

the blue

seeing

i see the world
in poetry

let
me
see

let me see with eyes of wonder.

eyes wide and
full of wonder
standing in the sunlit room
she watches as
the dust settles
finally, a chance, to bloom
the floors are empty
the furniture gone
the windows are closed
nothing lives here, anymore.
i wonder if she'd seen it
before
the way the light dances in
dazzling
not just through the glass windows
open
but directly from her soul

blooming.

the waves keep coming
one after the other
brutal
dumping, then
kind
gentle
and then,
brutal again
the cycle repeats
and i am caught in it.
i watch them from afar
i watch them from the shore
i brave them in the deep, and
i am grateful i am no longer
facing them alone

bravery looks like holding hands and not floating away.

the universe expands
on and on
blankets of
uncountable stars
i see them all
in your eyes

i knew from the second our eyes met that it was a meeting i'd like to hold every night for the rest of my life.

the way your eyes pore into mine

— delight.

we collide
eyes wide
hearts wild
like the way
the sea rages
and crashes
to the shore
that
my darling
is how
you crashed into me.
suddenly.

i have felt the collision of a thousand worlds all in the brush of
your hand.

today i woke up to the beat of a slow dance
i followed her rhythm
until the sun said farewell
and the sky turned dark
and the stars danced
to the rhythm
inside me.

i've been thinking a lot about sunshine lately
finding myself drawn to towards golden rays
even when life gets wild
i still see the rays of light
the colours in the sky
the colours in life
everyday is new
and i think the sun really reminds us of that, you know
it sets
it rises
everyday is new and the sky is always lit up
new
and so maybe
maybe we can be too.

tonight i walked home
the wind blowing my hair around my face
like the caress of a lover
and breathing deep
do you know what surrounded me?
flowers
darling
the flowers are blooming
did you forget?
the wind asked me
after the cold
after winter
the flowers bloom
and if that's the same for me
that's the same for you

your lips tumble over mine and
your eyes undress me
before your hands can even start to move
around me
your lips tumble over my name
they part in all the right places
move in all the right ways and
i am alight
under the gaze of
your delight
you set a damned *fire* in me.

rediscovery.

been taking the time to
notice
to see what the light does
when she catches in the trees
to see butterflies, birds
in places never seen before
colour and buildings and art
life —
i'm seeing it all
because i'm choosing to see it all.

don't live blind baby.

today I didn't play music
as I walked the familiar streets
to my familiar office
no, i listened instead
heard the steady beat of my heart
like feet on the pavement
one after the other
step step step
beat beat beat
i listened and as i listened
my god, i remembered
how it felt to feel the cold air
pierce my skin
like a needle sewing thread
i wove it all into me
every sensation
every moment i'd forgotten to savour
every word i hadn't said
another whisper as i beckon myself
closer still
you're alive baby
you're alive
listen,
do you remember?

i can see
more clearly
when i close my eyes
and
breathe.

your lips curve to answer
all the questions
my eyes are too afraid
to give away
i never thought i'd find this
i wasn't looking
i was just,
running
you stopped me dead in my tracks.
all that running
just to slam straight into
your steady gaze
i never thought i'd run into you.

i'll follow you to the place
where the sky meets the sea
i'll follow you to the place
where flowers grow, free

why do we seek to fill
all that we perceive
as empty
it is not empty
at all

but open room
free space

wide open spaces —
room to dance.

the raging

me

in the midst of the darkness
i felt a wildness rise up in me
a wild that i could only see then release
i carved it out into paper
ink spreading across white pages
the wild breaking free

everything is too much
until it isn't
and then
everything becomes a lot
until it isn't
and then some things are too much
until they aren't
and then everything is too much
until it isn't
this anxiety dance spirals and is filled with gentle reprieves
restful days and cheerful sunsets
and then the fiery chaos
and icy silence
of everything all at once
being too much and empty
empty and too much
and i am the centre of that fire-ice storm
i am the fire and the ice
i am the chaos and the silence
it fills me until I know nothing else
until i sink my fingers into the dirt
grab a handful of the earth
and remember
i can be this
exactly as i am
part of the universe
part of the earth
too.

i tore my entire world apart
to be here
to claw myself out of the grief and the raging
to learn to dive into the ocean
to make it *here*
after all of that
do you really think i have the energy
to spend on your approval?

i guess i just never saw the kids and the wedding and the mini van and the spending the rest of my life burning with wanting and watching as the fire slowing goes out and burns down to an ember. before you know it there's nothing but ash on the wind and empty places where wild once lived. **i want so much more.**

and i am learning to relish that wanting.

i remember every word
you told me to act
not on feelings
but to take control of myself
as though our feelings
aren't pointers
telling us how we ought to act.

baby if you take anything from this: listen.

too strong
and i am a bitch
too weak
and i am a woman
too strong
and i am a bitch
too weak
and it's my fault.

wear heels to the office
because to be taken seriously
a woman must be sexy
but to wear heels to the club
well, then it was our fault
for being sexy.

darling baby it was never your fault. darling baby you are
never too strong.

statistically
it is not
one woman
afraid
it is every womxn
afraid

statistically
we are less likely
to be held by the throat
by a stranger
than we are
from a lover father uncle brother friend

and they wonder why we don't trust them.

keys in hand
scream fire instead rape
don't smile
don't frown
don't talk back
why didn't you just say hello?
give me a smile sweetheart
why did you smile like you were interested?
look them in the eye
but don't make eye contact
make sure your friends know
where you're going
because
his don't.

a hand on my back
like you know me
own me
the entitled gesture
of a man
who has never
had to protect his body
from others leers
a man who owns
what he touches
and smiles as he touches me.

my god
this world
wants too much
from me
i need some fucking space to breathe

you
told me
i would be like the mountains
covered in the dark of night —
cold, unyielding
enclosed by shadows

but

i have learned to be/see/taste/touch —
light
i am the mountain surrounded
by starlit skies and heavens song

yes
i have learned the way of the earth —
after the night comes
blooming

there's rebellion in my blood
hit me once
break the skin
and watch the mad woman
pour out
i'll set fire to
the house that
kept me
held me
trapped me
and I'll watch as you struggle
to wrestle with my flames
watch me burn it all
baby
watch me laugh
the whole damn time

you'd need an ocean to put out this one.

i burned a lot of bridges, sure
and you always told me i shouldn't
but the whole time
i failed to see your fear
you need their admiration
so you keep your bridges, you play on all sides
but
i don't.
so i burned the bridges
watched the smoke rise to the sky
as it carried the ashes of the woman i used to be
i burned the bridges
because i don't need them
don't need the people on the other side of them
i don't need to carry the opinion those bridges
connect me to
so i burned them
set them alight
let the fire consume the opinions shouted
across the divide
i burned them because
i won't live afraid
i won't live like i need them.

why do we spend so much time fixating on what does not serve us? why do we put so much into "being" a certain way because society tells us to? fuck. that. fuck feeling like you have to be anything other than gorgeously who you are. fuck kids, fuck marriage, fuck careers - fuck any milestone that doesn't serve you. fuck the partner being your number one and only one. baby you are your own number one. why do we let systems of society determine our soul?

fuck it, i am my own greatest inspiration
i have burned away the skins that don't fit
let the smoke devour the thoughts
too small
for this wild mind
i have risen from the ashes
revelling in my the nakedness that remains
revelling in all of my self.

what could be more
divine
than that?

my number one lover is me.

i am the mad woman
the rebellious woman
the
you set me on fire
and watched me transform
into a fucking phoenix
woman
my tears have paved new paths
formed new river beds
and
i've burned men to ashes
with a gaze
i've sailed the oceans
as a dread pirate
and held captive
those who tried to hold me.

i'm a new woman baby.

she is fire moving through your very veins
burning all the words they said
she is the love you hold
when winter's turned the nights
to unforgiving ice
she is the one
you are your own

it took me forever to learn this, and i'll never let it go.

she is me
and i am her
i am her
and she is me
we are
one
and
because we are one
we
i
she
are
infinite

i've been drawing stars in the corners of all my pages / they re-
mind me that you shine brighter than any light in the sky

i will write love poems to my self if i fucking want to

sometimes when i stop
and sit still
i feel like i am
wasting time
and i realise
how deeply
i have bought into
the hustle culture
that says time is a
commodity
to be used
instead of
moments
to be lived.
i am human
i will not sell myself
i don't want to use time
i want to live it.

i thought once that the muse —
she was another person
or that maybe
she came only
in times of difficulty
of struggle
i believed that to write and breathe poetry
was to live a life of pain and
disconnect
but when i look at a city
alight with the glow
of the setting sun
i know
the best muse is joy
the best muse is me.

— *inspire your self. love your self. be your own muse.*

always i will find my home
in this body of
mine
and i will never be
homesick
again

we are the brave
the bold
the furious
we are the ones told
quiet
who are only now
finding out how
loud
we can shout.
we are the ones kept
small
taught to shrink and
twist and
contort ourselves
only just now
we are finding
the space we were born
to take
only now we are finding
the way our bodies
are made to move
move
and not
shrink.

of course we are angry.

woman
do not spend
another heartbeat
another fucking second
dulling your light
for the comfort of
others.

the cost is your self
and it's not fucking worth it.

the waves kiss the shoreline like a soft caress to the face
and I wonder how I didn't see it sooner
how I could ever miss this

love is not safe
love is not quiet
love,
love is *wild.*

getting ready to sleep
with a pen beside her bed
the ocean crashing in the night
she awaits the midnight call to dance
when the horn blows and the call comes
her fingers will be ready
to move freely with the gift of the night

create again.

maybe right now
life's taken a pause
because you need to
stop moving and
create space and
feel the sunshine
on your face
there is no right time
there is only now
there is only this moment

acknowledgements

to you, reading this book, i love you.
thank you for supporting this artist-writer and for wanting to dig into the feels with me. the support from my friends, family, and creative community have made this happen. the support of strangers on the internet always blows my mind. being here, with you, is everything

and to Jack, for taking me out to pizza to celebrate this book going live. i really like you and i really like pizza.

about the author

born in central-west NSW and raised all over, Jasmine Johnston has always had a love for a good story. growing up in Byron Bay and avidly reading every magical wizarding book that came out on day one, she fell in love with how we can find ourselves in words and stories – even when they're fictional. when she was 25, Jasmine left a rigid Christian space, sending her into a spiral of unlearning, re-learning, and connecting with herself. she found herself in so many others stories, and decided she wanted to keep giving language to experience, always. she see's a future rich with making art, writing more books, and creating space for people to find themselves through art. you'll usually find her sipping a black coffee (batch brew preferred) or a wine (red) or making her own negronis and having a dance in her kitchen. Jasmine is a creative writer & wedding and couples photographer based in West End, Brisbane. she lives in a colour-filled apartment with too many plants, her cat-baby Stormy, and her love, Jack. you can find out more about Jasmine at jasminejohnston.com.

www.ingramcontent.com/pod-product-compliance
Lightning Source LLC
Chambersburg PA
CBHW060022050426
42448CB00012B/2847